The Spe   of Dark

Ian   hig worke
in Engl nd and N   ore becoming a writer
and teacher of Creative   has held various
Fellowships, most recently as 2003 International Writer
Fellow at Trinity College, Dublin, and since then has been
Royal Literary Fund Fellow at Trinity and All Saints
College, Leeds. He has won the National Poetry
Competition twice and the Forward Tolman Cunard Best
Single Poem Prize, and received an Arts Council Writers'
Award and a Cholmondeley Award.

The Speed of Dark

Ian Duhig

PICADOR

First published 2007 by Picador
an imprint of Pan Macmillan Ltd
Pan Macmillan, 20 New Wharf Road, London N1 9RR
Basingstoke and Oxford
Associated companies throughout the world
www.panmacmillan.com

ISBN 978-0-330-44655-6

Typeset by SetSystems Ltd, Saffron Walden, Essex
Printed and bound in Great Britain by
Mackays of Chatham plc, Chatham, Kent

Visit **www.panmacmillan.com** to read more about all our books
and to buy them. You will also find features, author interviews and
news of any author events, and you can sign up for e-newsletters
so that you're always first to hear about our new releases.

'If I were called upon to name what spirit of evil predominantly deserved the name of Antichrist, I should name the spirit of chivalry'

— THOMAS ARNOLD

The Speed of Dark

Wallflowers at Beverley

i.m. Mike Donaghy

More instruments ring these walls than raised a roof
for God throughout all medieval Christendom;
stone arcades spring like dancers from the Minster floor,
keyed to their lord's calling-on song 'Da Mihi Manum'.

The Irish call the parchment drum this angel quiets
a bodhrán, though she lacks the ordinary beater:
Mike held his like a pen above the skin in wait,
counting on his own heart to inspire each tattoo.

But he might change to flute for quieter audiences,
bored without dancers' feet to ground his syncopation;
when he charmed them with Ruairi Dall's 'Give Me Your
    Hand',
they applauded and rose to the dash of his playing –

so Mike's book *Wallflowers* notes offbeat theories:
that we're all God's three-dimensional handwriting
or how a pin's head really can stage angels' ceilidhs –
another made dance the mother of all languages;

then it gives all 'This Living Hand', Keats' last poem,
which dampens my skin like the touch of a felt mute.
I'll sit out this stone angel till she leaves her drum,
raises and plays something quick on an Irish flute.

[3]

Moshibboleth

In Beverley Minster's stalls a teacher pauses,
halting his gaggle of exchange-school students
at a carving of a hooded fox preaching to geese:
'Foxes are common trickster figures in folklore.

René, your twelfth-century "Le Roman de Renart"
was forerunner to "Le Roman de Fauvel": even now
you'll see foxes run for their lives before horses
in all the Ridings of Yorkshire, "God's Own County".

To Native Americans, Joe, *Fox*, is *Coyote*'s brother
and a favourite incarnation for their skinwalkers.
Aki, a Japanese phrase used on answering the phone,
is known to be unpronounceable by fox-spirits . . .'

'Moshi moshi!' demonstrates Aki, proving he's human.
The teacher tries these words but becomes tongue-tied,
fails twice more. The mask slips. Red-faced, he barks:
'And this next misericord shows a fox hanged by geese.'

Fauvel's Prologue

Seigneurs et dames, you're welcome all!
I'm just flown in from Charles de Gaulle,
your man-stroke-horse-stroke-King Fauvel –
your interlocutor as well
with hopes my new verse may enhance
this show from medieval France;
like adaptations by Mel Brooks,
this show's based on my earlier books
with poems, music, illustrations
made when France was first of nations.
That's when its word for horse (like me)
inspired the code called chivalry;
this rode down Christendom's Dark Ages
with shining knights and shining pages
of rhyming octosyllable
which, disciplined and drillable,
would sweep all fields from its début
until your poets rode it too.
Four-footed lines, four-legged friends
delight French mouths – this taste transcends
sophistication in your tongue
which grunts like yahoos digging dung.
But please forgive my Jingosim!
Europe's seen enough of schism:
two Popes, you Prods; its left and right
took turns to reign as day with night
to chase some ism soon a wasm.

This I learned in Macrocosm,
capital of Lady Luck,
who raised me there from stable muck
to throne and crown and royal palace,
a Wonderland where I was Alice,
the first of many lucky strokes
enjoyed since from all kinds of folks;
from politicians, literati,
businessmen, the arty-farty,
churchmen, coppers, dons and judges,
civil servants – none begrudges:
all stroke and comb me just the same,
as 'fawn''s one meaning of my name,
they fawn upon my rough fawn coat
though smeared with filth from hoof to throat
with Dajjal's tar, oil, black bile, ink
and matter which some people think
good taste deems rather best avoided:
where would we be if that's what Freud did?
But also I'm a dirty devil
down at the sub-atomic level
where breed distinctions don't stay fixed
and hobbyhorse and arse get mixed.
I take this stage and human speech
to teach a lesson Luck would preach:
that crown and throne are soon thrown down
(my Lady's smile contains her frown).

And so that high I may still ride,
my aim's to make that dame my bride;
my plan to chain my world to hers (like
Geulincx's clocks become a bike)
propels this 'Roman de Fauvel'.
It has, too, Roman tales to tell,
for Rome's not fixed in time or place;
Dajjal's Al-Rum and mine roam space.

Right now, America's our Rome,
my rival stable-God's new home –
you ruled the waves: she rules the air
(and riding airs is work I share)
but now your naval empire's wrecked,
your tongue one Yankee dialect,
your politics a Trojan horse
or fig-leaf for her naked force.
If 'cheval' bore our chivalry,
our heirs the US Cavalry
ride helicopters to a fight
to show their Saracens what's right;
not doves, but locusts Scripture graces
with lion's teeth and human faces,
whirring wings and crowns of gold.
In your Good Book, my Sire's foretold,
a stablemate of Plague and War
and Famine; hence 'Venez au Cors',

my battlecry, excites the vulture . . .
But let me lead you back to culture,
where though I cannot make you think
you needn't: let your ears just drink
Fauvel's refreshed, refreshing song.
What horse's mouth would tell you wrong?

Dame Fortuna's Antilogue

O think, Fauvel, to mind your bounds,
I'm still the one who orders rounds –
of worlds and women, wine and song;
you're on an upswing – not for long:
male ends are things of squirts and jerks:
full female cycles rhyme God's works.
But now I'm turning on the jest
I made in crowning such a pest
who'd be La Peste à la Black Death,
King Claudius or King Macbeth.
This image of yourself's not real,
you're just a worm beneath my heel,
a phallic snack for early birds,
a hyphen hybridizing words.
You're less white knight to win my lips
than page of the Apocalypse,
preambling for that book of night
you hope your Antichrist will write.
You're king, for now, of shreds and patches,
a bit too keen to play with matches;
you spoke of teaching: soon you'll learn
your destiny's to crash and burn,
your only traces when you pass
a carbon hoofprint on our grass,
some carbon copies running wild –
a skewbald herd, half-foal, half-child.
In 'portrait d'encre' you've been limned,

a style reserved for those who dimmed
God's law, as did de Marigny
who rode a horse foaled by a tree –
he hanged for arrogance like yours:
you're both blood-brothers and blood-boors;
the overreacher's soul is crass
and black as was the Templar mass.
Your ink's black bile that blots this rhyme
to sign a melancholy time
the shade of melancholy humour,
grounding wars on lies and rumour –
O think, Fauvel, how this would pain
old world-transforming Charlemagne!
Fauvel, your foe is pure clear thought,
for darkness veils your upstart court,
you plot (as well as you are able,
ambitious as the Tower of Babel
when that rose and One God was young)
to rewind language to one tongue
while your tongue forks from pole to pole
like any double man in soul.
Now 'Macrocosm', as you call
in your new tongue my capital,
is more correctly 'Macrocosme'
in those true accents of our home;
but since you like your meanings double,
I'll serve a pun up for your trouble:

think Macrocosme like 'megabrush' –
enjoy your fortune while you're flush,
for soon my strokes will strip your skin
to glut my hounds upon your sin.
That glass now empty once was full:
like you, it's just a vehicle,
your words are here to carry tunes,
their light reflected, like the Moon's;
our audiences park their rears
to hear the music of my spheres,
not whinnying on life and art
from some high horse behind its cart.
Fauvel, cogita: you're a cog,
no more true king than was King Log,
a horseshoe charm hung from my fob,
so get that bit back in your gob.
You'd marry? I'll not fob you off,
I've someone here to share your trough –
Vainglory, my delinquent daughter;
if you're a rip, then she's a snorter.
'O who's the fairest of them all?'
she asks the mirror on her wall,
which fortunately can't reply
as mirrors don't know how to lie;
her face would stop a clock stone dead –
that's much like what you want, you said,
the power to hold back day and night –

and since you'll argue black is white,
then marry her in widow's silk
the secret blackness inside milk
(think Audiberti, not Renard,
as glossed by Gaston Bachelard).
I'd never wear your bridal veil
in nuptials beyond the pale,
since your name means 'false veil', Fauvel,
enjoy a marriage made in Hell!

Holme Ring

('Tribum/Quoniam/Merito')

I

'In sempiternum speculum
Pararare palam omnibus
Non pepercit patibulum.'

II

To reflect on this Anglian backswamp,
cross its low tide to Holme Tree Ring,
when the dead hang us from their footprints;

where circling alder pickets still guard
an oak's drowned heart, a blackened clock
stopped one spring before history invaded,

felled by grass ropes, raised here roots-up,
honoured by fire, prayer and dead kin
placed in its arms, buried in the air

to 'excarnate', scholars say now. These roots
nursed flesh of one flesh to bone of salt:
cradle, coffin, Albion's Fatal Tree.

[13]

III

'Fortuna raised a gallows
in the eyes of everybody
as an eternal looking-glass.'

Out of Context

An evil word is like an evil tree, torn from the earth,
shorn of all its roots. – Qur'an 14.26

A website glossed 'cleanskin'; his dictionary
of the Indo-European roots to English words
gives '*kers*' for 'black' (as fiery Krishna),
then '*kau*' for 'Caucasian' (those the sun burns).

'Ink' leads back to 'encaustic', so to 'holocaust'
but his page stays white; the light consumes
each verse he turns out like some failed Keats
when he pictures the red trees of human bombs.

At last he turns to that Tree of Hell *Zaqqum*,
its scalding fruit the shape of demons' skulls:
this the damned must harvest, gorge and abuse,
which tastes, the Qur'an warns, 'like dregs of oil'.

love me little

on the school ranch holidays

hands called me/ *slo mo, echolally* & *veg*

when it rained & we/ had to play cards & i repeated what they said,

went out of order & twisted when i was bust. but

they got nice in time,

talking with me in the sun

as   i   bounced   round   the   paddock   on   ponies.

teachers,

on the other hand/ were always telling me to REFRAIN

from saying this/ &/ that that

i shouldn't have.

(hands don't

hiss/ REFRAIN so much as shout/ DUMBSONOFA

when i let stuff out/ i shouldn't have

like secrets or horses).

dumb, i got to love words &

where they rode in from. *refrain*

's from the latin for/ *bridle* (not my path

i've found) & means:

a recurring phrase in a poem or/ song. i found when

phrases recur in poems or songs nobody got angry,

so i got to love them too. *burden* is another word for *refrain*:

love me little, love me long:

that's the burden of my song

a ranch hand sang (he called me his burden). a hand's song. a poet's
singing hand: leaves in keats'.

teachers told me my/ mind was all
over the place, that i/ had no
     CENTRAL COHERENCE.
now i'd reply/ that if i twig leaf
not trunk it means my thinking is
     not 'arborescent' but

'r   h   i   z   o   m   a   t   i   c'
   & in poetry i surely know/ my pot8os &
       if i'm slow/ my vegetable love
shall grow/ vaster than empires.

     i showed you my hand(s):
     give me your hand.

Behoof

'Girl number twenty unable to define a horse!'
said Mr Gradgrind for the general behoof

Quadruped. Graminivorous.
Forty teeth. Sheds coat in spring.
Siege engine. Saxon land art.
Ritual bride for Celtic kings.

Height in hands: workers' symbol.
Slaveboss. Hero. Heroin.
Frames for flogging, clothes and timber.
A cheat's translation crib.

Rosinante haunts windmill crankshafts
greased by rendered hackney.
Lottery ticket rented daily.
Norse Horse of Day: Skinfaxi.

Norse Horse of Night: Hrimfaxi.
Emblem from the Catacombs.
Curry favour = curry Fauvel.
Curried language. Currycomb.

Lucky Chinese Year for poets.
The poem's id, in Lu Chi's verse.
Freud's client, hippophobic Hans;
Pfungst's Clever Hans the Counting Horse.

Counting Gradgrind, mad and sad grind.
Pegasus: knacker's fat.
Hack for taxi, tack for Faxi.
Brass facts. That's that.

'Use Complete Sentences'

French oral practice: Teacher's nervous look
to where I stand in turn and raise my book:

'My father has grey horses on his head . . .'
She snorts. Her face grows dark while mine glows red.

flogging dead brains for something true to say
when Dad's grey horses took my breath away:

they took the air to run rings round the sun.
Now (with a crib) I work through Yang Tzu-yun,

where horses were his metaphors for breath.
These sentences are sentences of death.

Communion

Once, for our 'Preparing for Communion' class,
a young nun on teaching placement screened
'The White Suit', a Vatican Film Unit rental.
In the lingering cold of that Friday afternoon
with a distant, circling angelus of ice-cream vans,
the mote-thick beam of our chattering projector
lit Giacomo and his subtitles' pale translation
on the pock-marked wall of the school gym.
Only ten, like me, he was already sporting
the holy ghost of a handlebar moustachio
which quivered with the passion of his pleas.
But his hot Italian could not melt his mother,
a widow just too poor to afford a white suit
for Giacomo to wear at his First Communion.
To save for one, he worked nights at a foundry
only to lose his right arm down the fiery throat
of some ancient malfunctioning ore converter.
Then, to God's circuitous design, his workmates –
communists themselves converted by his faith –
stump up for cloth and the hire of a tailor.

The film ends with Giacomo in Milan Cathedral,
empty white sleeve pinned to left silk breast,
swanning to the altar-rail and smiling bishop,
who waits for him with the chalice and wafer,
through billowing incense which bleaches out
all subtitling as if dumbstruck by the vision.

During break, I grew a moustache of free milk,
chalked hosts on tarmac and blackboards,
pictured my father's Guinness, Alec Guinness.
But most of the class had weeks of nightmares.
Parents complained. One day, without a word,
the nun was gone. To me, she'd never been
quite there, less real than Giacomo's moustache,
my phantom limb itching in its flesh impostor
or my grasp of sacramental transubstantiation.

Travelling Exhibitions

I *'Scultura Lingua Morta' at the Henry Moore*

A true sculptor, wrote young Martini,
works to order, like making shoes.
Just flying horses wear them here
from when Il Duce ordered boots.

The *Monument to Army Marksmen*
by Morbiducci aims too high;
Marini's *Mounted Gentleman*
at Yeats' grave keeps passing by;

here, Arpesani's *Fascist Victory*
triumphs down the arches of the Gallery,
a hollow angel cast from heaven
and wartime economy national alloy.

The legend to Fontana's bronze
quotes the Ode to him by Sinisgalli:
a photograph of a bas-relief
soon rendered down for artillery.

Last Martini's *Hero of Africa*,
gives its subject Airman Minniti
(beheaded by the tribe he bombed)
a martyr's loincloth and bare feet.

Sculpture, wrote the old Martini,
is a dead language, beyond repair,
not made to last. Even without rain,
crowds paralyse the Henry Moore.

II *'The Art of White' at the Lowry*

Escaping rain with my new husband, he pauses before
Sugimoto's photograph of a drive-in movie screen;
the artist exposed his film for the precise duration
of the main feature, freezing the speed of light
to absolute zero inside a numinously empty frame,
illuminating cars like the suitcase of uranium
from *Kiss Me Deadly* echoed in *Repo Man*.
Bored by Zen reflections, I'd clap one hand,

imagining the fugitive colours as fugitive Polanski's
seminal *Chinatown*, his film noir turned film blanc.
Grounded in his negative take on that LA ghetto,
Faye Dunaway plays its China White-skinned heroine
addicted – as Polanski in life – to cold love. Two lookers.
Jack Nicholson is the private eye out of his depth,
flawed as Dunaway's iris which he notices too late,
his first suit white enough for a Chinese funeral.

Polanski's vision persists past Marina Abramovic's *Hero*,
showing the artist on a white horse with a white flag;
the Flake White on Lowry's seascape flaking off,
then Zineb Sedira's *Self Portrait, or the Virgin Mary*:
all but her eyes hidden behind a ground-length veil.
At *Chinatown*'s climax, Dunaway is shot through her eye,
hunted down by her father who's also father of her child
(John Houston, who'd later make *White Hunter Black
    Heart*).

Dunaway's Chinese gardener laments her saltburnt lawn
to Nicholson, saying splashes from her ocean rock pool
are 'bad for the glass'. The private eye then reflects on
what might have splashed. They fish out broken glasses,
Dunaway's drowned husband's, their lenses scratched
to frosty webs, to skaters' pediscripts on thin ice.
At Picasso's *Dove* my husband polishes his own.
I ask him if he's seen *The Spider's Strategem*.

Et De Man Sale

Nowadays we are less than ever capable
of philosophical generality rooted in genuine self-insight.
– Paul de Man, Introduction, *The Selected Poetry of Keats*

The fascist regime grants
complete freedom to the poet.

To his motto, grant crest and mantling;
pard coward under an escutcheon
showing one hand dexter on a shield,
cuffed sable, in vambrace damascened;

couped at the wrist, gloved in argent
stained murrey sanguine and apaume;
between thumb and forefinger proper
his sinister eye, just plucked out.

What Is The Speed of Dark?

A song in this lyric tradition . . . was less likely
to have a measured rhythm the more the poet
sought to achieve the high tone
– Christopher Page, 'Tradition and Innovation in BNfr. 146'

White night. Fauvel in his palace:
melancholy blacked-up Claudius/Hamlet;
high-strung, wrung-withered, restless
despite the silence. Bad dreams.

The walls of Fauvel's Elsinore
(inscribed with deviant, false music)
close in. Crush notes. Bars of 'Love's Prison'
with staves as blank as Ritter Glück's.

Du bist mein glück, du bist mein stern.
The air bites. His heartbeat flutters:
his Lady love would stall him once again.
She tells him he knows no measure,

would have him harp upon her daughter.
You cannot call it love. Pawn sacrifice.
White Queen checks Black King. No mate.
Fauvel cannot temperately keep time.

Fauvel Love Song

('Douce dame débonaire')

Follow your bright love, unlucky shadow
    whose comeliness is black
    from sun borne on your back –
yet follow your bright love, unlucky shadow.

The sun can quicken as she seems to stand
    a seedling Campion,
    that shadow's champion;
the old hand followed with this second hand.

Shadow with your hand, unhappy lover
    then close round your own dove;
    be dovecote, nest and glove:
what light has veiled, let darkness now uncover.

Discover what man most loves is himself:
    be warmed by your own sun
    in loving number one,
a love that will not leave you on the shelf.

Turn your gnomon to your source of light:
    the fall awaits the proud,
    for all of us, the shroud;
so come like God, alone, and in the night.

Chanson de Charlemagne

('Alleluia, Veni Sancte Spirite')

Laisse I

In old geste assonance I raise this song
for Charlemagne, that royal paragon
now at the right hand of the One True God
until France's need should again prove strong.
Once, he was disinterred at Pentecost –
when the world most fears Antichrist's assault:
the mere show of his bones saw that threat off.
Our wise first Holy Roman Emperor
would know instantly Fauvel was false
as the music on Fauvel's palace walls.
But Charlemagne could use a lust-crazed horse,
as wittily sentencing Ganelon
who sold the pass and Roland to Muslim dogs:
he had him tied between four stallions
then a mare freed to frisk and draw them on –
quartering him for his quarterless plot.

Laisse II

Wounds made a dovecote of our Saviour's flesh,
so those who give wounds are the Dove's true friends.

[29]

Charlemagne was the man to take revenge
on those Paynim hordes for brave Roland's death:
leading his Franks against these infidels,
his sword Joyeuse sliced through helm after helm
till, like broken rosaries, scattered heads
rolled where Tencendur his horse trampled them –
through hot blood this cold blood skipped gay and fresh,
fit for a king in this world or the next!

Laisse III

As Christ again, to French verse rhyme must come;
as Giraudoux writes, 'Rhyme is the best drum'.

Laisse IV

Having brought the *racaille* to their knees
and gaoled a bunch of them for their treacheries,
the heir of Charlemagne played with his keys
in the Garden of France, taking his ease.
He watched zephyrs sport in the liberty trees,
thought with his wine some salty snacks might please,
perhaps from his local fromageries –
when de Gaulle's spirit whispered on the breeze:
'Two-hundred and forty-six kinds of cheese . . .'

Menocchio Uncowed

They hauled me in for idle thoughts
I shared about Creation –
like Hildegard's fourth vision,
drawing on cheesemaking:

our World turned from primaeval milk
whey seas and God like curds;
its white made Day, its blue our Night
while angels grew like worms.

My theory reached the Inquisition,
souring its big cheeses
for suggesting something rotten lurked
in the lineage of Jesus.

Banker, cardinal and prince
the inquisition cowed –
even Galileo once
turned around its power.

Banker, cardinal and prince
the Inquisition fear:
imagine mine, a country boy
still wet behind his ears.

But time saved my philosophy
although my body burned:
like milk, angels, verse-ends, worlds
and jigs, a worm must turn.

Mummers

(Earsdon, 1913)

Their Doctor of Potions feels sick.
St George (with their squeeze-box) is late.
Their Captain's been hitting the drink.
The audience aren't going to wait.

With pit-pony strigils for swords,
tin-whistles to squeak out their jig,
red hoggers, white shirts and blue weskits,
they've iron-soled clogs to sound big.

Blacked-up like he'd come straight from work,
their Fool wears a huge pair of drawers;
his hair is the last sheaf of corn:
it tips back his head and he roars:

My mother you burnt for a witch,
my father you hanged from a tree;
but now I'm the sword-dancers' Fool
and who will dare meddle with me?

His calling-on song starts their play:
the audience quivers and quakes;
the publican mouths all their words;
his little boy shivers and shakes.

And next year they'll tremble no less
at the song in another Fool's throat
when this year's is dancing in France
to a whistle with only one note;

where the boxes they brought aren't for music –
like the Captain, they always keep mum;
where St George rolls up pit-pony eyes
and the Doctor of Potions can't come.

The Spit

My father wore the wicker horse-head
on Stephen's Days to drum the furze
from house to house with the Emly Wren Boys
to sing for milk, eggs, pence or bread.

On Christmas Day I turned the spit
and burned my finger, it hurts yet . . .
between his finger and his thumb,
he tasted everything to come:

he wrote it down with a pig-horn pen
filled with beestings from a hen;
he fanned it dry with a horse's feather
plucked on a day without any weather.

Another day he plucked my hand,
a dying man in London Town;
he told me what he'd written down
but couldn't make me understand.

Between my thumb and other thumbs,
I lose the jig's time on my drum;
the band lose patience. I head home
to turn my father for some poems.

The Price of Fish

For love of my Methodist boy,
in Fishermens' Bethel I stood
to mouth their strange Wesleyan hymns
with one verse that changed me for good:

Ah: lovely appearance of death!
What sight upon earth is so fair?
Not all the gay pageants that breathe
Can with a dead body compare.

The wound in the side of their Christ
was the womb of the bride their men sought,
and bright were the children they'd raise,
and right all the ways they'd be taught;

for death to them had little sting
since hard work so calloused their fears:
they drowned all the fires of the Fiend
in blood and in sweat and in tears.

But the warmer I grew in my love,
the less did I trust in their Lord;
I read of that trawler from Hull
gone down in the Isa Fjord.

I fled from my Methodist boy,
but tell his name under my breath
whoever I'm with for some warmth
in a life like the wrong kind of death;

through wrong kinds of nights to find peace,
I pass all the wrong kinds of ships
with wrong kinds of bands on their decks
for the wrong kind of song on my lips:

Ah, lovely appearance of death!
What sight upon earth is so fair?
Not all the gay pageants that breathe
Can with a dead body compare.

Coda

A gill-net once was custom-made,
a hand-tied web of mortal hemp;
now modern trawlermen believe
in nylon monofilament.

Electrospun, invisible,
a knotless mesh, this matchless shift
will cast no shadow but a spell
to check and catch the breath of fish.

Should one break free, being overfull
or torn by underwater tides,
it sinks, so bottom-feeders glut
but when picked light, this net resiles

to rise, to fill, then sink, then rise –
shape-memory may fish for years
that never-never land of plenty,
the shelvy deserts of our seas.

Every country calls these 'ghost nets'
whose factory ships still vex the deeps,
and each such net's a magic tongue
whose syntax makes words disappear.

Midriver

French inventor Louis le Prince who lived in Leeds shot the
world's first moving film on this bridge, storing in light heavy
traffic on hooves and tyres; below, as busy a river unreels
past the Dark Arches, the station, Salem Church – a
methodist kaleidoscope in black-and-white stained glass,
sober reflections still on consumerism's glitter. *The sword,
the sword is drawn: for the slaughter it is furbished, to
consume because of the glittering* – Ezekiel's vision, wheels
within wheels.

. . . *here is temporarily who I am*, goes Mike's 'Midriver', his
London Bridge sonnet, who was a bridge: Irish-American,
poet-musician; he was one of we hyphenated people, flesh of
our too too solidus flesh. But I felt in his work's shadow,
brilliant, with epigraphs in the original French – from Char,
for example, in 'The Palm' where Django Reinhardt bunks
with 'P. De Man'. Mike looked and laughed like the star of
Amadeus; in the B-movie, *I Married A Smog Monster*, as
northerners call citizens of Middlesbrough, my wife's home.

But I can still remember the first time I saw this River Aire,
an obsidian mirror of chemical waste that tanned drowned
animals, changed the sex of fish – even developing film, a
local photographer told me. I picture him gently immerse, lift
out, then clip to these railings weeping sheets *the charcoal-
black old family snapshots burn* (Mike again), a gallery of
veronicas in oils where the same face echoes in mirrors

[39]

reflecting mirrors, a little smaller every time. Beside Tetley's Brewery now, a new developer's vision –

faux wharves and warehouse flats – rises on its yeast. But unreal Leeds now traffics principally in cyberspace, with clean rivers but a light-pollution problem instead. Like this architect, I'm over-given to quotes – to prints, not the originals like Mike, his French or Louis le Prince. *Under thy shadow by the piers I waited; only in darkness is thy shadow clear.* Is that some hymn I heard from Salem? My wits are setting fast. Even this half-light grows thick. The Dark Arches are closed because of a pier failure.

DE SENECTUTE

although i'm now senile
at least i'm not senile

Eye Service

('Quasi non ministerium/Trahunt/Ve/Displicebat')

'Trahunt in precipicia . . .':
'they back us up against the edge',
our ministers who've sold their doves;
they play the markets with our lives.

Knights Templar turned to moneychanging
when Salem fell: our money's changed
to cards as plastic as the surgeons
in our new temple of the body.

All hymnboards there are fixed on 'I',
that economic truth of Latin,
both number of our Decalogue
and capital of our god's kingdom.

No motets praise the Trinity,
our choirs just babble monologues,
each lyric 'Je' *sans frontières*,
in every town the only game.

We're turned from People of the Book
to people of the bookmaker;
a dark brigade, our horses dark
we'd never stake on Pascal's Wager.

'*Qui nos tenenetur regere*':
'those whose duty is to rule us';
'*Pensantque lane pecium*':
'may think upon the price of wool';

'*Et non currant de ovibus*':
'whose thoughts don't run on us, the fleeced';
'*Ve qui gregi deficient*':
'woe to who sell out their sheep'.

The die is cast in Caesar's Palace;
slot-jockeys, we're on Fauvel's string,
our silks all spun by Saadi's spider,
our race the sport of a one-eyed king.

Faujjal

('Garrit Gallus/In nova fert/Neuma')

'In nova fert animus mutatas
dicere formas draco': 'Again
they say the soul shape-shifts,
now into the form of a dragon'

Fauvel changes in the light like dollar ink
from bill to buffalo to skinwalker witch,
from pig to palomino to Dajjal's pale mount,
crossing next into the Dark Messiah himself.

Dajjal is the one-eyed Antichrist of Islam,
named from a phrase for an old con-trick;
blacking over injuries on camel's skins –
the same brush tars our own bête noir Fauvel.

Dajjal's a hypocrite with more than two faces,
his triple-tyrant nature being at once human,
institutional and a global virus of ideas,
money talking every language like his music.

On US dollars, a pyramid with thirteen steps
rises to Dajjal's eye; thirteen, number of coven,
silver-tongued Judas at Jesus' Last Supper
and Usura's Knights, the Templars' Armageddon.

Dollars have thirteen olive leaves, olive berries
but thirteen arrows in its war-eagle's claw;
there are thirteen letters in E Pluribus Unum,
battlecry of the first and all Romes, al-Rum.

But thirteen will prove unlucky for Dajjal,
King Without Clothes, denier of God
whom prophet Jesus will soon destroy,
then all the world's pigs, then its crosses.

'*Garrit Gallus flendo dolorosa . . .*'
'The cock crows, sadly weeping';
'*Coram Christo tandem ve draconi.*':
'Woe dragon, to face Christ at last.'

This Graft of Verse: Closure

The figure cut by one famous poet, a Christfox
in leather trews, seeded in me the itch
to write myself. I consulted the experts:

they cobbled me a poet's mind, an anthology
of xenografts, shreds and patches: tailor's
cabbage, translating it into their own language –

POEM: *Pre*-Osteoblastic *Egf* repeat protein
with *Mam* domain. I came to grasp irony
and sub-texts in the basement membrane zone.

Christ is like a book inscribed on the skin
of His Virgin Mother; Bersuire's image tickled:
had that priest not lost Christ's Prepuce

From the shoebox he was keeping it in,
new machines can now read the DNA
from the offcut of a ritual circumcision,

then mill lengths of second skin to order . . .
but for Christians, the other lines of Abraham,
like certain poems, finish just a bit before

Book Match

Lost in a parallel translation of Catullus' poetry,
my brother, I find you again; bright as in childhood,
deader than Latin, in that corner of my mind
forever now lonely Bithynia, with the poet
laying out his gifts before his brother's grave.
My brother, poetry occurred to me after you
could object. I know we swore we'd be footballers
but I lacked the art. Anyway, I offer no laurels
but a wreath of cuttings – 'murdered darlings' –
gifts so intractably themselves they won't play
by the book. O how I've laboured to contrive
plausible contexts that I may plant such flowers
as Browning's use of 'twat' for a nun's wimple;
for the name of the Swiss John Bull, Colin Tampon;
for St Scholastica's Day, when Oxford rustics
massacred over sixty students of its University;
for Keats' Cortez on Darien, really Balboa;
for ancient Maya, who, when too drunk
to keep down any more of their booze,
pumped it up their arses; how in Catullus' Rome,
certain breaches of its laws entailed a similar
introduction of radishes and mullets' fins.
He would have been as disgusted with our 'haitches'
as Arrius', but Catullus, too, was unsophisticated
in swallowing the myth of great British wealth
as once some Irish. We found its silver spoons
being counted faster and faster by their owners

the closer we got to their canteens. My brother,
do you remember the night we copied that trick
from some old comic book, how we rolled an egg
between two wooden spoons above a candleflame
till its shell was thickly velveted with soot?
When we lowered it into a glass of water,
before the saucers of our eyes it vanished,
its place instead taken by a silver ghost –
and how unimpressed our mother was by magic,
impressing this with the two wooden spoons
on the striped eggs of our winceyette behinds?
But please forgive me, my brother, I can see
by your quick gesture that I've crossed the line,
gone out of play, so you pull the disappearing trick
that you got off to such a fine art so long ago,
with that slo-mo fade like the Roman fresco
on the cover of this book: Horus, a child
with his forefinger lifted to his lips – O,
all right then: like a cheeky striker taunting
the incadescent fans of the home team
he's just scored against. A good away win,
my brother. Till the rematch, hail and farewell.

Brilliant

*What Yeats does . . . is to help to create a sense of restored
community.* Edward Said, *Culture and Imperialism*

Everything in Leeds is Brilliant. Kaiser Chiefs

I met him one brilliant day
coming with brilliant faces
from clinic at number 12a
on our way to more brilliant places.
Then, riding a bus into town,
I sorted the world out with Sid –
agreeing when all's said and done,
we said a lot more than we did.
And then we lamented the sport,
remembering better times bitterly
and how they were only too short.
All changed, changed utterly.

This bomber's Dad ran a chip shop
which fried not with dripping but oil;
on match days he stood on the Kop
with Sid, now Sidique, from the school –
they wrote his work up in the *TES*.
You'd think you knew what Sid dreamed
he showed such social-consciousness,
so sensitive his nature seemed.
But drugs had this other young man,

till his parents sent him to learn
at a madrassa in Pakistan.
He too has been changed in his turn.

You ask where's our sense of community;
we have to make do without Yeats,
but some would say Beckett Street Cemetery
embodies its spirit and state.
Across from the clinic, grass grows
on Dissenters' and Anglicans' Walks,
Recusants' and Missioners' Rows,
on lost plots for Baptists and Catholics,
fading shades of the Christian dead –
though the provisional wing of the meek
did firebomb the mosque up the road
after London, then stone some poor Sikh.

Just words are the aims of these stones
marking common deaths, those from fires,
old wars, a few mining explosions.
This one is Red Tom Maguire's
who brought down old City Fathers;
it's green as his family's home
(he rode Yeats's wingèd horse)
or the mosque's polycarbonate dome –

you can sing Tom's lyric 'Feller Hand'
to 'Graves are the Mountain-Tops
of a Distant, Lovely Land'.
Brilliant. This is where our bus stops.

+ve /s

At the Melancholy Clinic –
a prefabricated Skinner Box
in the car park of our hospital –
I'm filling in a questionnaire. CBT:
I am this/that, I feel ill/well
etc. deleting where appropriate.

Sometimes my steering wheel locks:
it's all the either/or that bothers me;
my negative capability chokes
into existential paralysis.
Rumi hits the Jungian spot:
like the shadow, I am and I am not.
At least Transactional Analysis
recognizes positive strokes.

Civilization

Let no one to the marriage of true minds
raise barriers or admit impediments:
love is not love that alteration finds
for bishops, governors or presidents –
Bush claims 'our fundamental institution'
is somehow by your wedding under threat,
then seeks to tamper with the Constitution.
His Press Room echoes like a minaret.

I stretch the metre of an antique song
that your true rights may shine through my dull ink,
for poets sometimes do stand up to wrong
if not as often as we like to think.
But if I lie, then Shakespeare couldn't scan,
no woman woman loved, nor man loved man.

Freed Time

Rock'n'roll is a story written in black and white
– Sarfraz Mansoor, *New Statesman*

Who coined   'Rock'n'roll'?
Al Freed   first said it!
Thirty years   before Freed
poor blacks –   no credit.

No tick   '. . . around the clock'
Big Bill   Haley sings:
white face,   white hands,
white key –   black springs.

Bucks flee   black bands,
cash down   black hole;
Leonard Chess,   cheque mate:
Chess Records,   bank roll.

Spector   haunts them next
to raise his   Wall of Sound:
more singers,   more strings.
White wall,   black ground.

Skins' Soul,   Ska, Reggae;
rock mix: Two-Tone.
Specials'   'Ghost Town'.
Rico's   trombone:

out, in,   in, out;
roll, smoke,   rock, roll;
fired, hired,   fired, hired;
dole, job,   dole, dole.

Clock on,   clock off;
pub, club,   dive, shebeen;
ticked off   on tick:
black ghost,   white machine.

'Walk the Line'

In the second of his autobiographies, Johnny Cash
traces the roots of his family tree all the way back
through Queen Ada to Duff, 'first King of Scotland' –
duff history. But Duff is from Dubh, meaning 'Black'.

At a turning point, inspired by Nashville evangelist
Jimmy Rodgers Snow, the 'Man in Black' would write
what proved Cash's only novel, called *Man in White*,
about the conversion of Saul to St Paul the Apostle.

Cash's late 'Bon Aqua' guitar, made in Nazareth,
PA, inscribed him as 'Johnnie' and was bound
with black and white celluloid. Now hagiokinema
rhymes truth with spellbound legend, life with death.

He wore black, he had sung, 'for the poor and beaten
down/living in the hopeless, hungry side of town.'
For my line, I took his gospel message and bent it
out of true to break images. I think he meant it.

Variations

The Gaelic bán in English means white or fair-coloured
– J. J. O'Connor, 'The Irish Origins and Variations of the Ballad
"Molly Brown"', *The Canadian Journal of Traditional Music*

Snow-white Molly Bán,
taken for a swan,
shot in a storm
by her snow-blinded swain.

He struck out his eyes,
soon was found hanged
not by her father's
but by his own hand.

Her name rode the waters,
so did her song;
their coffin-ship docked
in Harbour Breton.

My lover in Canada
said there she's called Brown,
shot dead in rain,
taken for a fawn.

From poetry's ghosts
roots of words spring:
our mouths tumble corpses,
Emerson sings.

Bán also means blankness,
nothing, no tone;
the colour of silence,
snow melted by rain;

for nothing's as fair
as the swan's fatal air,
never heard here,
never heard there.

Mencken Sonnet

According to BBC2, the etymology of 'cocktail'
is lost. Horsist purism. See Thackeray:

'I can't afford a thoroughbred and hate
a cocktail.' Mixology. But the dry martini

seeks a pure strain again, its French vermouth
dying out like harmonics of the lost chord:

Dean Martin just had waiters mention it nearby;
Churchill merely bowed in the direction of France.

Buñuel, lifting an image from St Thomas Aquinas
for the mechanics of the Immaculate Conception,

talked of a ray of light falling through Noilly Prat
onto the ardent base spirit of the gin in its glass.

I myself simply watch sloe gin evaporate slowly
for the infinitesimal vibrato in the air above.

Fauvel's Fountain

('Hic Fons')

No *unda purificans, aqua regenerans*,
still less is Fauvel's stinking Fountain
the grail-gold wellspring of eternal life,
a crystal-brimming cistern foamed with pearl
by ordered play from some Le Nôtre centrepiece;

it's a sump gushing ordure, a bog
for a John-the-Baptist to the Antichrist,
volatile as air-fuel or fertilizer spills,
a burning slurry like the water of Dajjal
scorching the sweet Garden of France's lawns.

Those plashing about in this gargoyled trough
are not the scum of the earth, but its cream:
fat of the black milk of human unkindness,
gawping at their reflections on its skin
poxed by guttering squirts from Fauvel's jet –

a shape-shifting Cloyne-tar-water tree of death,
its self-delighting emissions bitter on the tongue
stuttering upwards dizzy high from its Latin root
to the crude Anglo-Saxon ejaculations erupting
from Fauvel, lord and font of all bad language.

Fertile as cancer cells or plague bacilli,
Fauvel's very colour fawn's from *fetus*:
his melancholy brood flood from the lip
of his cistern towards Paris, already baptized
in *aqua degenerans, unda damnificans.*

Last Round

('Ci Chans')

I love this motet:
its names seem to clink:
'*Ci Chans Veult Boire*',
'This Song Wants A Drink'.

The French and the English
are rarely in sync:
here, both tongues hang out,
being after a drink.

My song's Fauvel's coat.
If rougher than mink,
it still warms your throat
as well as strong drink.

Top up from his Fountain
for though it might stink,
its tar-water cocktails
are healthy to drink.

(For why shite's artistic,
please talk to my shrink –
the horse knows the way.
He'll go for a drink.)

'*Hic Fons*' makes us hic
as black bubbles blink;
in a glass darkly,
this song wants a drink.

Fauvel gets blind drunk,
but a nod or a wink
will catch his red eye
when he wants a drink.

Fortuna's blind
as love in the pink;
now snookered on black,
she too wants a drink.

With fortunes, as curtains,
what rises must sink
so sink some rounds now,
this song wants a drink.

Ignore your watch; it's
later than you think.
This song's calling time.
This song wants a drink.

Rider

You like poetry? I'm not reading your mind,
just your diary, where I note you've put me down
as 'Sosostris'. Bit of a card yourself, sir.
Oh: so this appointment's just research?
Then let's see what I can conjure up
by way of facts. Our oldest surviving tarot
is the quattrocento Visconti–Sforza deck –
from Prospero's court, sir, if that helps.
Though the Church banned cards for gambling,
she recommended tarot for moral instruction,
as Calvino would again for plotting novels,
calling it 'a machine for telling stories'.
Check out his *The Castle of Crossed Destinies*
with Crowley's *Little, Big* and King's *Dark Tower*
where his Man in Black reads Roland's future.
This Rider deck's the product of adepts
of Yeats's Golden Dawn, but coloured later,
tailoring its suits to Querents' skin-types –
you're Swords, also for the element of air.
First you must shuffle. Slowly. Four times.
No: nothing to do with Templars, anagrams
of ROTA, TORA, Sephirothic Trees of Life
or '*tar-ro*', supposed Egyptian for 'royal road'.

The drawn blank: your Significator card. We turn
the Chariot drawn by one black and one white sphinx.
Some see here Cathar dualism, Descartes des cartes.

What do I think. Of course I think yes and no.
Wheel of Fortune: Douglas writes that this beast
was once equine, as if turning a gin-wheel.
The Magician (or the Cobbler in Italian packs)
reversed, suggesting mental illness, black bile;
this Ace, black gold and one-eyed merchants. Death,
a Yorkshire Rose with 'XIII' on his banner. Ends.
Beginnings. Depends. Nothing's that black-and-white.
These tarot cards are mirrors, not windows.
Does my reading disappoint? You think me
a hypocrite lecteur. Forgive my little joke:
I can be a bit of a card too. As above,
so below. Or as the Sufi have it, sometimes
the man on the saddle: sometimes the saddle
on the man. This isn't only research is it?
Mid-life crisis? You feel yourself trapped mid-
stream, with no sign of another horse
for that change which is as good as a rest.
And you want to know more about the rest?
The rest is . . . sorry, that's your fifty minutes.
Shall I book you another disappointment?

Swineherd

('Porchier mieus estre')

I'd rather be a swineherd than his swine,
his swine before the Jew who won't eat pork,
a Jew before the Moor who won't drink wine –
I'd rather walk the walk than talk the talk.

I'd rather I was uncorrupted text,
not remixed by some jumped-up yellow hack
and meaning one thing but then half the next:
I'd like to get this poet off my back.

I'd rather be the horseman than his word,
fight a Templar than carve up his purse;
I'd rather I was feared than I was heard.
I'd rather I was dead than in this verse.

Notes

But thou read'st black where I read white – Blake

The 'Roman de Fauvel' is an early fourteenth-century cycle of satirical poems and songs in two languages (French and Latin), in two books and surviving in two main versions, the later and longer of which (BNfr.146) formed the ground of my commission for new poems to be performed with original songs from Edward Wickham, director of the Clerks Group, a vocal consort specializing in pre-Baroque music. Updating the text's concerns proved eerily straightforward, for as Eco has written *all the problems of the Western world emerged in the Middle Ages*, and Armstrong *During the Age of the Crusades the West found its soul.* Tuchman's history of this century is titled *A Distant Mirror*, and if it did not seem that distant, I often felt I was entering a looking-glass world in researching this Age of Chivalry. For example, one of its founding works of literature, the 'Chanson de Roland', recasts Charlemagne's rearguard ambushers at the end of his Spanish expedition from Basques to Arabs, while immediately after the Madrid bombings the Spanish government attempted the reverse; Bush sought Muslim allies for a 'crusade' that much Christian sentiment opposed, with the West's original desire to preserve access to the Holy Land's wellsprings of God's grace being exchanged for that to oil.

Beyond the general corruption of contemporary French society's governing institutions, the cycle's immediate targets include the ambitious royal counsellor de Marigny and the Knights Templar, the latter having been recently suppressed for supposed idolatry. Along with the imminently expected Antichrist, both are associated with the anti-hero, usurping man-horse Fauvel whose name is an acrostic for Flaterie, Avarice, Vilanie, Varieté and Lacheté, also suggesting *faus-vel* ('false-veil') and fawn, a colour of evil narcissism. Elevated by Fortuna, Fauvel seeks to marry her in order that he might avoid inevitably being cast down again by her wheel. However, Fortuna palms him off with Vainglory, from whose marriage to Fauvel spring the numerous *Fauveaus nouveaux*, which overrun and defile 'the sweet Garden of France'.

The central image of the corruption of the rich in the Roman is their constant stroking and currycombing of Fauvel's filthy coat, which is ultimately the source of the English phrase to 'curry favour'. Fauvel's reign marks the Age of Melancholy, the humour of black bile. Porter has described the Western medieval debt to Arab scholarship in this area and the humours were even associated with the four strings of the Arab lute.

For a work and time obsessed with the Antichrist, I borrowed from Arab tradition the figure of Islam's one-eyed Antichrist Dajjal, who will ultimately be slain by Jesus in the region of Iraq. A trawl of the Internet will reveal perceived connections between Dajjal, Templars and George Bush (though these sites change quickly and are subject to security monitoring). The etymology of Dajjal's name recalls Fauvel's coat and like Fauvel Dajjal sought (according to Smith and Glasse) *to stop the cosmic wheel from turning*, as well as being the source of beautiful music, a feature of the End of Days.

The overriding assault of the 'Roman de Fauvel' is on hybridity, distinction dissolved, things becoming what they should not. This is reflected in its visual art, where in a subtly coloured manuscript, there are thick, *portrait d'encre*-style outlines which evoke *more moralizing and serious didactic works. Rather as we today enjoy certain genres of film in black and white such as film noir* (Camille). However, BNfr.146 is itself multiply hybrid: between words and images; words and music; in music, between Ars Antiqua and Ars Nova, as well as systems of notation, some of which include the patterning of blank spaces; the shifting and

[68]

unstable forms and rhythms of its songs; as samizdat/high culture artefact and so on. Dillon describes how in it *song operates differently from its sonic realization* and how in handling its pages *as flesh meets flesh, skin mingles with skin . . . readers also, literally, become part of the object.* It was my experience and I hope will be yours too, that like the cursed videotape in Hideo Nakata's *Ring*, even copies and other versions can restart the cycle.